trains of winnipeg

trains of winnipeg

poems by Clive Holden

LIVRES
DC
BOOKS

Printed and bound in Canada

Edited by Jon Paul Fiorentino and Robert Allen
Book design: Clive Holden, Clint Hutzulak, Richard Hunt
Cover design: Clint Hutzulak
Filmstills & photos: Clive Holden

National Library of Canada Cataloguing in Publication

Holden, Clive
    Trains of Winnipeg : poems / Clive Holden.

ISBN 0-919688-59-4 (bound).—ISBN 0-919688-57-8 (pbk.)

    I. Title.

PS8565.O4143T73 2002   C811'.54   C2002-904179-1
PR9199.3.H548Y73 2002

The publisher and author gratefully acknowledge the financial assistance of the Canada Council for the Arts, SODEC, and the Manitoba Arts Council.

DC Books
C.P. 662, 950 Decarie
Montreal, Quebec, H4L 4V9, Canada
www.trainsofwinnipeg.com

for Alissa

Thanks to Elizabeth and Martin Holden, Clint Hutzulak, Richard Hunt, Jon Paul Fiorentino, Andrew Horridge, Christine Fellows, John K. Samson, Jason Tait, Steve Bates, Ricardo Sternberg, Gilbert Dong, Bonnie Light, Sean Virgo, Robert Allen, and Molly Peacock.

Twelve of the poems in this book were first published on the audio CD, *Trains of Winnipeg* (2001), which is available from Endearing Records or Signature Editions. Others were first published in *Matrix Magazine* and *Dark Leisure Magazine*.

The rest of the *Trains of Winnipeg* project can be seen and heard at: www.trainsofwinnipeg.com.

1 : condo

2 : manitoba manifesto

3 : burning down the suburbs

1

condo

condo

i dreamt our car was towed
away, our dirty Toyota
from my parents' luxury condo
parking lot—what the hell did it mean?
we've driven that car
all over the country
back and forth and up and down,
and my parents are one place

we have this house
now
and are trying to live
in *one place* and our dirty car
isn't gone, but just takes us to the lake
down the road
or around and around this muddy town
we fell in love with
and we've stayed here and pitched our mortal tent
like all the others
under the tan western sky

my parents' condo
is where they've moved to die,
they'll never move again,
except to space, heaven, the eternal ether
and the gracious ground wet and pungent
with millennia of crushed bone
and weeping piles of leaves

their condo
was built to be unusually strong,
immovable, says my engineer father
who watched its construction and approved
its earthquake-proof
quality material materiality—
it has a wide and sturdy stance
like a giant glass and marble headstone
marking all of our graves for us—
and the clean black parking lot's
curved on the top of a hill,
the land rolling down on all sides . . .

on the following night
my wife dreamt we were refugees,
we'd been forced to move
to a post-hippie luxury enclave
on an island off the West Coast—
either we'd been torn from this place
by tragic circumstance,
or we just forgot that we'd stopped moving,
and went one move too far

the coastal trees gleamed
like angry white children
in the expensive yellow sunshine,
and we walked
together, bent over, in utter
misery

18,000 dead in gordon head
(a found film)

i found an old vhs tape recently.

it was an edit record of some film footage i shot in 1985 in a suburb called gordon head—where i was a teenager.

i'd projected the film onto a white wall and re-shot it with a camcorder so i could log without scratching my only print.

but i never finished that film. the footage was lost—it was thrown in the garbage by an angry roommate. she was pregnant and wanted the room in the fridge for her free food from the clinic and bags and bags of white milk. i guess she thought she was justified—i was on the other side of the country at the time—it's a long story. she was a *tester*. she'd test to see if you got mad and if you didn't she'd keep on testing you until you got mad—and i never got mad back then. i was proud of it. i used to say i could always see *the other person's side of the story*.

then—she—threw my film in the garbage.

ᛋ

i started to make the film after witnessing the murder of a thirteen-year-old girl. she was shot by a sniper in the neighbourhood where i grew up.

i even lay on my side on the road where she died. i don't know what i expected to feel. empathy—sympathy? but it was just hard concrete.

i filmed the split-levels, service stations & the air raid siren over the old gordon head store—while my friend andrew drew in oil pastels. we talked about the light there on misty rainy dusks—even though it was just a suburb.

i was across gordon head road, getting out of my 1964 pontiac canso in my old friend dave's driveway.

i heard a *crack* that bounced off the houses. it wasn't like a tv gun shot. it was like hearing a | thin | fracture | form in the rest of the day.

and as i looked up at the girl with her friend (they were barely teenagers in their little jean jackets, laughing hysterically and poking each other on the way to my old gray-block high school down gordon head road) she suddenly jerked her head to one side and fell forward— down and down—she hit hard and skidded on the gravel shoulder and i thought it was strange she didn't put out her hands to break her fall. some cars stopped and a businessman with slicked hair and a red tie crouched beside her with his man's hand on her little moving back and i ran into dave's house to phone the ambulance.

i argued with the operator because there was no 911 in our city yet and i couldn't find a phone book but she wouldn't connect me or give me the number until i started yelling at her right into the phone that i could SEE OUT FROM DAVE'S SECOND STOREY KITCHEN WINDOW straight down to the girl's still writhing body. her friend bending over covering her own face with her little bird hands bending low low her mouth opened.

and then she connected me. and i stood and watched and my old friend dave there beside me wondering—what.

after a while two ambulance vans came but she'd already stopped moving. the four men all-in-white went inside a van with the girl for a long time—but finally, three of them exited slowly—two got into the

other van and one got into the driver's seat of her van, and they backed
and turned. and drove away without lights.

and i kept thinking—why doesn't this feel more unusual.

i mean, i'd already seen it. thousands of times on tv. *over* 18,000
times i read once in a magazine.

(18,000 deaths by the time you're 16)

but this was real and i didn't feel anything different. yes, i felt dead like
i was in shock. but that was the same deadness i always felt—except
when i was drunk and felt the panic and anger from feeling dead all
the time. or did i just think i *should* feel angry or horrified or terrorized
at the way things were—with the nuclear end of the world, ronald ray-
gun, sky-blue chevrolet wagons and all those families in all those silent
houses.

i used to hit things back then. i punched power poles, and thick doors.
the pain felt—right.

for the rest of that day i'd suddenly remember what happened.
and feel guilty. i thought it was wrong to think about other things, but
i just couldn't keep my mind on it, it would move away.

(i wanted to think something important about it.)

it was in the headlines and people all over the city talked about it. on
the sidewalks and in restaurants—it really affected them. *nothing like
this has ever happened here* they said. and i'd be at the next table but i
wouldn't say anything. just get up and leave.

and at work it turned out i was in a hair-trigger temper. four days after
it happened my boss looked at me and i realized i'd been yelling at this
guy for no good reason. and from his expression i knew—and he said
gently, *why don't you take a couple of days off?*

so i went to long beach with dave and we camped and i tried to cry by talking about it on the sand by the fire with the waves rushing in at me and out again into the dark—and i did cry for just a second and it felt a little better.

§

a few weeks later i went back to school out east, and i might have forgotten about it except i kept witnessing violence for the whole next year, little things like rounding a corner on a down-town sidewalk and stepping into a pool of blood with no one else around, thick and dark red stretching from the building to the curb.

or a fortyish woman running in front of a car below the school cafeteria windows. the hollow metal & stuffed pillow sound of her body hitting the hood, her head knocking-in the windshield and her being thrown ten feet and lying in a curled still lump.

and two teenage boys in a knife fight behind the supermarket with blood spraying in little drops on the white cement and them still circling. a crowd of kids with books in knapsacks watching and

not moving. and my feet walking me quickly away like it wasn't happening.

and the jumper on the subway. the screaming train brakes and the doors suddenly slamming open and a woman at the front on the platform screaming on and on like she was stuck inside the train brakes bleeding from my ears and echoing off the plastic tiles as i ran up the escalators as fast as i could panting-panicking and finally into the cold sunlight gasping for space. and I walked for miles in the cold that day.

and in a rich mall a middle-aged man in a mackinaw had just jumped from the upper tier of the sparkling glass atrium—was lying in my path as i exited the subway and rounded the orange juice kiosk on my way to class. i almost stepped on his face. i stood there as he lay staring up at me with one bulging red-soaked eye and the side of his face mashed in and crimson. and i turned and walked away but not too fast. like a criminal trying to look cool—winding through the crowd trying to find the *goddamned exit.*

and finally, there was the motor-cyclist in the intersection outside my apartment late at night. i ran and put a blanket on him because i'd heard that's what you should do. but i made the mistake of looking inside the little window of his helmet. his round gold-framed glasses were shattered. he was smashed and he was gone. his girlfriend stood in the middle of the street gulping for air and hugging herself. tight like he used to—strong but soft after lovemaking.

§

it stopped then. or i stopped seeing so much of it.

and i shot this footage. i even lay down with the camera on the side of the road where she lay dying.

where she died.

18,000 dead in gordon head

(stills)

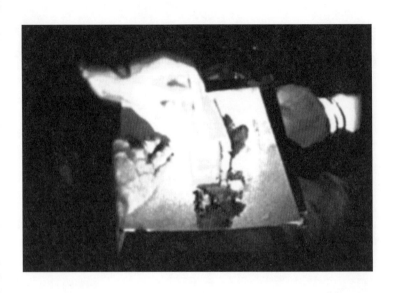

Cocktail Party

cocktail
party

cock
tail party
cocktail
party cocktail
party cocktail
party   cocktail
party   cocktail
party cocktail party
cocktail
party
cocktail party cocktail
cocktail party cocktail party
cocktail party cocktail party cocktail party
cocktail party
cocktail party
cocktail party
cocktail party
cocktail party
cocktail party
cocktail party
cocktail party
party
cocktail party cocktail party
cocktail party cocktail party
cocktail party cocktail party
cocktail party cocktail party
cocktail party
party
cocktail party cocktail party cocktail party
cocktail party cocktail party cocktail party
cocktail party cocktail party cocktail party
cocktail party cocktail party cocktail party
cocktail party cocktail party cocktail party
cocktail party cocktail party cocktail party
cocktail party cocktail party cocktail party
cocktail party cocktail party cocktail party
cocktail party cocktail party cocktail party
cocktail party cocktail party cocktail party
cocktail party cocktail party cocktail party
cocktail party cocktail party
cocktail party cocktail party
cocktail party cocktail party
cocktail party cocktail party
cocktail party cocktail party
cocktail party cocktail party
cocktail

cocktail
party
cocktail
party cocktail
party cocktail
party   cocktail
party   cocktail
party   cocktail
party   cocktail
party   cocktail

party cocktail

party

cocktail
party cocktail
party   cocktail
cocktail party cocktail
party cocktail party cocktail
party cocktail party cocktail
party   cocktail party cocktail
party cocktail party cocktail party
party cocktail party cocktail party
cocktail party   cocktail   party
cocktail party cocktail party cocktail
party cocktail party cocktail party
cocktail   party   cocktail   party
cocktail party cocktail party
cocktail   party   cocktail
party   cocktail   party
cocktail party cocktail
party cocktail party
cocktail   party
cocktail   party
cocktail   party
cocktail   party
cocktail party

20

The Jew & the Irishman
(a comic)

When I was sixteen my parents insisted I stay upstairs and serve cocktails to the women they knew from the university, their significant husbands, a psychologist from our street and a lawyer in his desperate kilt . . . like market surveyors, they asked polite questions about what I liked and what my plans were for the future.

I poured them triplets, the only way I knew how to drink, from thin plastic McDonalds cups with friends in my Chevy II wagon with no back window . . . I'd had a better car but creased it on a power pole at the bottom of the long hill to the bay, with my cartoon-handsome and tragically talented friend Anthony, we walked home and sobered up with instant Nescafe, phoned the police from the rec room two hours later, and strolled back to wait . . . I told them there were no injuries, just my confession . . . and no one came out of those houses, or even looked out a window from across the street, or from the cedar split-level five feet from the pole that I'd half broken through . . . the street was deserted and wet with my useless car bent double, it was very quiet as we sat on the trunk, having shared our first wreck.

My tall, beautiful father, who never said much at home, stood with the lawyer and a publisher and another engineer, and one of them said, "Did you hear the one about the Jew and the Irishman?" The Jew was greedy and untrustworthy and the Irishman was a criminally stupid drunk, and my father's face turned from its usual descended black cloud to charcoal red, his mouth opening at last like a thin, hidden vent in a volcano, and he actually said something, and they were burned by his words . . . after twenty years of those jokes, in Victoria . . . and they stepped back, the White Anglo Saxon Protestants and their reasonable facsimiles, and filtered away from my parents' new

L-shaped living room with the small oak tree inside (for luck) and the floor-to-ceiling windows . . . and I loved him.

Later, I stepped to my window to look at the moon, which wasn't owned by any of them. My father, who was rarely drunk, stood with his sports jacket open on the flat stone patio, one foot on a planter ledge, and he looked up too, smiling like I'd never seen . . . we gazed together at the free moon, and he seemed without gravity, for once.

dogs running
(a super-8 film)

dogs running

dogs wagging their liver tongues

dogs smiling yellow fangs at the silly wind in their fur

dogs twisting and tumbling like ragged men down a straw hill

dogs' feet turfing brown clods of strangled grass

dogs mounting :

dogs launching into the green air
dogs weightless fumbled grace
dogs flipping end-on-end
dogs crashing terrible thighs and proud chests

dogs running dogs running dogs running

unbreakable bones

my mother and father are very beautiful,
full of *beaux gestes*
and handsome profiles against the sky,
i love them
and they're very old and joke of dying

i had a cold when they visited
our home in winnipeg
i was afraid they'd catch their death,
i was afraid i'd kill them
with a microbe as small as the universe,
i am afraid of the size of the universe

my mother and father have style and natural dignity
come from pain and passion
that moved them across the world,
they cut a fine figure
like a clipper on the western horizon
you can just see their masts now,
their hull has gone below the rim
proving the world's round

i love them
and they'll never leave me,
my lovely dad always promised me
he wasn't gonna die,
and my mother's guiding hand
in the philosophies of the world
will live in me and in my atoms

and in every hand i shake
and in the juice
of every tree's leaf on this,
our parent earth

my mother and father are home
again as their vitamins kept them alive
for now,
they deserve a few peaceful years
if deserving something's
a concept we're allowed
on this plane

i love them,
and i'd make wide and strong
            wings
for them, if i knew how,
with white mottled feathers and
            unbreakable bones

rhyming method

rum, i am here on earth due to the rhythm method
the rime on the roofs of nanoose bay
the supercooled fog wrapping the wooden walls
on christmas week, '58
glazed hams and egg nogged to the brim
my parents said (yes) let's rumble

as the robed man in rome
paying no attention to the ruined curtains
drank wine from his round chalice,
nibbled rye from his stone bowl

the labour choir sang, *ottava and terza rima,*
the holy snakes writhed in a mating ball
dreaming deep in rem sleep
remembering dimly their animist pasts
they murmured: *the devil is in the details*

three tines toward heaven
a dead ram floated down the tyne
past the newcastle mine where a black shaft collapsed
and the coal wives ached and ran rheumy

in downtown manhattan
the lion took a room with the lamb
and in jerusalem they memorized rambo,
singing, *procreate ad rem, procreate ad rem*
rhyming men, rhyming men

nanoose

I saw a deer in our backyard
they tell me I wasn't born yet
there were red apples on a tree
ragged crab-grass and dark woods beyond

there was rain, years of rain
the apples glowed mottled crimson
growing in the moistened air
and the sky was the colour of angry sand

my family was on the balcony with me
my doe-eyed sister and old-eyed brother,
my parents in each other's long arms,
and two more like me watching from beyond the rail

Nanoose Bay is my family's birthplace
the deer showed us how to run away
and how to stand still in a startled meadow
in the mystery, where the apples hung

nanaimo station

i was born in nanaimo two blocks from the station
three from city hall and a block from the church
dad drank black coffee in the malaspina hotel
and mom was a dark-haired beauty of the amateur stage

i was born in nanaimo two blocks from the station
a red and white seaplane flew low down the passage
skidding down the harbour to the floating dock
on the milky blue glass of the water that day

i was born in nanaimo two blocks from the station
the mining shanties and the downtown reserve
the family motel on the road to victoria
and an rcmp cruiser winding through town

i was born in nanaimo two blocks from the station
on a wet and cool september 23rd
in a town of water by a forest of giants
the branches hung heavy with silver for all

i was born in nanaimo two blocks from the station
the booming grounds full of stripped-orange trees
trussed by a man in a small metal boat
whole forests from the inland mountains laid bare

i was born in nanaimo two blocks from the station
at the corner of fitzwilliam and kennedy streets,
it rained for sixty-nine days without stopping
the fog clung to buildings like old women's hair

i was born in nanaimo two blocks from the station
my family was perfect then, no one was sick
the country was new then and so were we then
the food was like magazines and the cars were all big

i was born in nanaimo two blocks from the station
the steps to our house were covered in moss
but our family was shining from moving and moving
we went to the station and didn't return

active pass
(radical poet on his fortieth birthday)

walking onto deck, wishing to hell i still smoked,
i peer beyond the ferry's tethered bow and below decks
to a clanging b-train stretching its length inward,
a family of peering faces in a mini-van
and cartoon bright compacts filling the last dark gaps.

the giant pneumatic doors grind to life, meeting to form a hulk against
the salt sea wind air.

submarine shudders from mount engine:
we quietly ship from the slip, sterning and waaarning,
we flat across the strait of someone else's dead king,
shouldering past the rump of a robin's egg blue korean car freighter.

leaning on the wet steel railing, staring due north
at the government's new super coal port,
and a ten mile charred line of ore cars
drawn against the royal blue horizon
shuttling forward to cough up their dead weight
onto the multi-storey mounds of ashen rock,
under a black tangle of cranes and tall straight pipes sea water
gushering in foam-white plumes that arch, fall and land
flaccid and spent, settling onto the quiet, smokedust beds.
the tracks stretch inland to canada's opened spine,
the rockies montana and the black-stained hills of idaho.

the people's new super ferry enters active pass
horn horn-ing to the little boats
to GET OUT OF THE WAY,

the ship lolls into the gun-metal S
a giant watery snake laid in a wide V of sodden rock.

. . . to the passengers on the outer deck, the ship's whistle will sound while
transiting active pass . . .

i'm halfway there. after all the foreplay,
teenaged end-of-the-world angst, young adult fictions
and petty fights with pretty tyrannies,
the decay of the body's systems is in full-swing.
the rudder's slightly bent, but knows the way by now.
the driveshaft has vibration problems, but still spins bright.
the doomed engine runs day and night.

. . . an important safety announcement . . .

so much activity in one, eye-closing, passage
one rocked and fir-shadowed crease
in the great divide between sea and sky.

upstairs on the bridge the ship's toy men masters
play at the steering wheel. in the cafeteria,
i listen to the islanders complain about unfair fare hikes,
but the corporation knows by now
the mainlanders will always pay to get even closer to the sun,
the ferryman can charge whatever he wants
for this rough crossing,
this rain-soaked passage.

. . . life jackets are stowed in specially marked boxes . . .

i squirm in my hard-ass mcdonald's chair
watching the tourist wet dream pass beyond the windows
like flat TV screens,
their copyright bought last year by disney.

then the bus driver leans to ask me,
hey, what do you think's on the other side?
we both look to the waitress
who wipes the table in ever decreasing circles,
probably, she shrugs, *the waters where we started?*

—a final shudder from well below
as the iron whale lolls again to port side
god's great tongue licks the reefs into white foam
the coffee vibrates in my mortal cup.

rain memory: vancouver

we painted our window frame metal flake gold
everyone in vancouver should do this as the gray light
and the dark of the constantly dripping holly
framed by this window became a celebration of two million muted

lives, once it rained for 97 days
the streetlight remained on through morning and afternoon,
day meant the gloom lightening
for a few hours, then giving up into sodden evening

again, but it was a special time for us living with our golden window
it's true we almost parted ways
but it was our first real home
the challenge of which was daunting, vancouver

was like going into the pain
and finding a man in a suit the colour of a wet sidewalk
handing you a bill for all the pain you've caused,
but we rode away, we left that fish-coloured cloud behind.

slaves at lions gate

i'll be your slave and brush your slippers
if you'll tell me why you wanted her to jump

i'll paint you in cream and cut new berries
if you tell me how it felt to watch her fall

i'll bring a naked siren to your ear
if you tell me if you watched her waving hands

i'll oil your underbelly and smooth your thighs
if you tell me when she broke her back

i'll lick your furrowed brow and shop-worn hands
if you simply tell me what you are

i'll kiss you on your mouth to try and wake you
if you tell me why she had to cross the strait

i'll cleave a wet, new rose for you
if you admit—that you, too, want to fly

hands of henry moore
(for two voices and a murmuring crowd)

moore
mammal
mammalian . . .

there's a sculpture in the
new wing
of the vancouver airport,
green jade emerald seaweed green
haida or classical,
and the kids used to run to it
and climb on it
so it was different each day,
they were shifting light
from the window in the roof,
until the signs went up—
me, i think we should touch it
i think we should all touch it . . .

moore
mammal
mammalian . . .

art makes its bedfellows
serves the institutions of power
(the institutions of power)

like an airport, where you rarely see the flightless poor,
but we can touch it
we can climb it like apple trees,
piles of rusting leaves,
ignoring the owner's signs
because we are mammals in our own right,
so we can touch it, because
we are mammals, remembering . . .
we are mammals, remembering . . .

moore
mammal
mammalian . . .

i want more,
i want *knowledge*
i want to touch henry moore's hands
i want to kiss the hole at the
            centre of the universe
i want my mother's giant hips
and i want the other
too—i want the sun
too—i want the sun
too . . .

moore
mammal
mammalian . . .

2

manitoba manifesto

manitoba manifesto:

: i see everyone's children with enough food, and love. i see everyone's children with enough food, and love.

: look, at the rain, on the wires outside.

: *we're dying here, there's not enough food and YOU don't care! we're dying here, there's not enough food and YOU don't care!*

: the earth, flesh and bone . . . the earth, flesh and bone . . . the earth, flesh and bone . . .

: now this woman is serving you, getting you your fork and your dressing on the side . . . she's *serving* you . . . where's the nobel prize for that?

: i'm tired, nobody loves me and i want to go home.

: don't sell your soul to *anyone!* don't sell your soul to *anyone!* don't sell your soul to *anyone!*

: *the bison are all dead and we've fenced the deer. the bison are all dead and we've fenced the deer. the bison are all dead and we've fenced the deer.*

: look at my hands, they've worked hard and they're scarred.

: LEAVE the freak show if it's wearing you down. LEAVE the freak show if it's wearing you down.

: here's a photo of a baby, and the mother of all mothers.

: hey, i need twelve bucks for a ticket to the pas.

: forgive yourself if you can—forgive yourself if you can—forgive yourself if you can—forgive yourself if you can.

: it's the sound of the wind in the leaves of the trees   it's the sound of the wind in the leaves of trees.

: so, if the universe is infinitely big, then it's also infinitely *small* . . . so that must mean that i am both infinitely big, AND really, really small.

: look. i love you. i really do.

: i said, we're on the surface of a rock hurtling through space! i said, we're on the surface of a rock hurtling through space!

: (listen: in sierra leone they live for 25 years, and we survive for 75.)

: the fortune teller told me, go scream in the woods. the fortune told *everyone*, go scream in the woods.

: cars . . . and the engines of despair. cars . . . and the engines of despair. cars . . . and the engines of despair. cars . . . and the engines of despair. cars . . . and the engines of despair.

: could you just hold me . . . no, no sex, i mean . . . just *hold me*, please, tonight.

: i am so tired . . . of not going home with you.

: *don't buy it for one minute! don't buy it for one minute! don't buy it for one minute!*

: are you really ready . . . for everything you've always wanted?

: be as kind as you can be . . . be as kind as you can be . . . be as kind as you can be . . . be as kind as you can be.

: *take the train, across the prairie, and stare out the windows, at the shifting patterns, of light and dark. take the train, across the prairie, and stare out the windows, at the shifting patterns, of light and dark. take the train, across the prairie, and stare out the windows, at the shifting patterns, of light and dark.*

: my anarchist neighbour said, POVERTY IS VIOLENCE. it was written in big letters on the front of her house.

: my anarchist neighbour wouldn't lock her doors, or license her dog.

: the cage door is open now . . . but we're afraid of the change. the cage door is open now . . . but we're afraid of the *change*. the cage door is open now . . . but we're *afraid* of the *change*. the cage door is open now . . . but we're afraid of the change.

bus north to thompson with les at the wheel

les, driving the bus north to thompson,
told us of the blood-drunk manitoba mosquito,
weaving across the highway
like a tiny fat mayor of a town that's about to die,
after feasting with friends on the flank of a half-crazed and galloping
moose in the deep woods
and wheeling off with her pungent mother's lode,
fatally weaving in front of the bus to thompson . . .
sudden and hard as glass
she's spread akimbo like a crazy cubist crucifixion,
legs bent in opposing, sharp-kneed angles,
a shattered thin-boned swastika
from the gathering movement in all insect world,
but best of all was the round circle of red,
the size of a canadian dime.

les, on the following night driving south from thompson,
said his favourite was when a cloud of fireflies
died communally all over his windscreen,
and more incendiary cousins collected there
as the free sun disappeared in a burnt crimson wash over the black bog,
if he could make it through the reserve without the kids smashing his
rear windows with their ancient rocks, after flashing his rooftop lights
at the passing church-bound train,
and everyone was asleep and the moon rode high
and full of mother's milk
that poured down into the bulrush ditches,
and spread along the length of the 88 mile straight-away
north of moosehorn,

where he switched off the headlights,
and the firefly torsos glowed for hours after their deaths,
together spelling new constellations
to be read with great care.

De'ath in Neepawa

I didn't expect to be moved by your gravestone
After all, you're nothing but words now
And a few old bones.

Do you feel at one with the cosmos, or ultimately alone?
I heard you say *yes*, at the ford in the river's flow
I didn't expect to be moved by your gravestone.

Writing is old magic like tarot or rune stones
Did you read the leaves from your giant brown betty,
       or were coins thrown
And a few old bones.

I whistled, taking shots of the De'ath family headstone
My dark haired wife and her dark-haired friend
       moving like angels in a row,
I didn't expect to be moved by your gravestone.

On the way home on the Yellowhead we saw an old blue roan
Dancing in big steps, all light & air
And a few old bones.

I loved seeing your Corona in your museum home
But it was your dark gaze from a 50 cent postcard that took me.
I didn't expect to be moved by your gravestone.
And a few old bones.

saigon apartments

the nights we rose from a lovers' sleep
to our windows, peering through the venetian blind
fumbling limbs, still gaining consciousness:

a woman's running skreeel

or merely,   *crash*—
a crude thud and splintering safety glass

or two men squaring in the black back lot

or the deaf lovers' quarrel, hands clashing
in brown half-light, gesticulation
damned denunciation hanging in the air
their *heard* voices like feral cats, wounded
keening, gutteral and pleading to *pleauuuuse!*
be let in, more naked than any skin

or the demi-prostitute from saigon apartments
next-door, screaming, sore again at her semi-pimp
suburban boys in ball caps outside her groundfloor
their headlights waiting, her prized blonde tresses
thin white dresses and drunken gait and wail

love in the white city

love in the white city . is impossible
the streets are too wide
and the wind has rows of perfect teeth

love in the white city . is unlikely
the mud is too deep
and the snow tastes of dogs

love in the white city . is farcical
the roofs are too slanted
and the sky is frozen solid

love in the white city . is laughable
the buses are so slow
and trucks circle the city, roaring all night

love in the white city . is horrible
in february my cat leaps at shadows
the poets fire guns at noon

love in the white city . is impractical
we're too kind to eat flesh,
the handle's broken off

love in the white city . is a mortal sin
the beds creak like swings
the river's too deep and too old

love in the white city . is a TV crime
arrest me on camera
brush me with your blue baton

love in the white city . is a poor excuse
the summer's too violent
the spring is barren

love in the white city . is lamentable
that building's full of rich men
and that one, african amputees

love in the white city . is a tragedy
with dancers in black costumes
and a continuous mechanical drone

love in the white city . is ridiculous
the natives all know
they'll take it back one day

love in the white city . is unreachable
the chimneys have tried
the ice fog billows and swoons

love in the white city . is forgettable
a cloister of gray nuns
aching to recall

love in the white city . is a nightmare
we're running down main street
with red clothes and singed hair

love in the white city . is a mystery
where has my youth gone? asks the mayor
as the gravel trucks sift by

love in the white city . is distasteful
they do it in bushes
on dry leaves and on grass

love in the white city . is illegal
i explained all my poems
so they buried my books

love in the white city . is a marathon
the sun is too yellow
the trees dwarf our tiny cars

love in the white city . is too brutal
the horses mount cows
the chickens eat pig

love in the white city . is near-silent
my eyes froze together
i can't . . . hear you

love in the white city . is blasphemous
i will hunt you down
and kill your new wife

love in the white city . is graffitied
on all wooden bus benches
and young women's fur coats

love in the white city . is cancerous
it grows in the dark
in tidy black flowers

love in the white city . is moribund
a quick death under the bridge
in murder's north capital

love in the white city . is for sale
hard cash for soft breath
a whole district for exchanging seed

love in the white city . is motorized
large men in pick-ups
watching women in vans

love in the white city . is in orbit
two ugly lovers
walking slowly in air

love in the white city . is hard as rock
the bird song is bitter
the rain hammers down

love in the white city . is unlovely
your face on a matchbook
your hands on my back

love in the white city . is dangerous
take my hand, hold my head,
weep with me to sleep

love in the white city . is expensive
you've cost me everything—
i have nothing but you.

trains of winnipeg

i am a train of winnipeg
i've had no home till now
i hurtled north and east and west
and flung my song to crowds

i am a train of winnipeg
for years they couldn't hear
the longing song i sung for them
their hands spoke of their fear

i am a train of winnipeg
my roaring engine, steel and wheel
the fire-the crash-the size, my hands,
the way the driver feels

i am a train of winnipeg
i'm coupling ice and field,
and mountains, lakes and coastal rains
i asked for you and kneeled

i am a train of winnipeg
your branches, switches, spurs
steer me to the sky and back
i'm driving north, i'm yours

i am a train of winnipeg
we lie on gravel beds
i cross and cross your river arms
your legs, your dreams, your head

i am a train of winnipeg
the sun plays on my yard
on your wide streets and dirty stores,
churches, parks and bars

i am a train of winnipeg
i love to taste your food
your parents brought you from afar
you're salty, sweet and crude

i am a train of winnipeg
i will *never* leave
i'm parking in your station house
groan, and gasp, and heave

i am a train of winnipeg
i'm wintering in you
i'm embers in your winter glove
(each day your skin is new)

i am a train of winnipeg
you're geese on steel-white sky
your V follows me overhead
charcoaled on my mind's eye

i am a train of winnipeg
i've had no home till you
your dress, the wind, your tangled hair
my rail on track is true.

where would the lines be drawn
in the *event* of war?
well, the war against the weak
wages in the air around us,
hanging like my poor roommate in his bedroom cell.

neighbour walk softly.

where are the lines drawn now
in your relief map of the neighbourhood?
well, *they're* over there
beyond the new fence we've built with drugstore razor-blades,
their rented limbs, and our new bloodless technology.

neighbour walk softly.

where would you draw the line
if you were told to choose
who goes to the bowels of the stadium
and who wins a new car!
well, they're coming for you now
with feathers and shovels, have you thought this through?

neighbour walk softly.

what line would you write as a promise to those left
behind when we garbage this planet for another?
well, i'd promise to serve my country
on a platter to the rocket scientist who builds the ship
that takes away the line-writers among us.

neighbour walk softly.

i said, where did you draw the line?
when we slaughtered the 200,000 desert-faced young men in the gulf
and cleared the homeless with horses and water cannons,
did you bed down at last with the man on TV
who said for god's sake, *hold the line*?

neighbour walk softly.

would you line up for bread for a day
if there was a loaf for every child?
well, the lines are humming with the news now,
we're killing them softly and skillfully
in long lines, against the neighbourhood wall.

neighbours walk softly
(stills)

what is a cherry blackbird in the sky
what is a man's machine spilling his seed
what is an idea buried in soil
what is a sprout inside your mom, the earth
what is a seedling fearful in the world
what is a young plant now, *i'm green! i'm green!*
what is a shaft of gold, long and longed for
what is a swaying field, a swaying field
what is yellow arrowhead of grain
what is a swather swathing low and wide
what is a combine, teeth and wire and loud
what is a farmer's daughter in a truck
what is a granary, a storm-dark sky
what is a grain train rolling three miles long

what is across the line of distant hills
what is a freighter's hulk at sea, a port
what is a mill and flour virgin white
what is a baker's van at 2 am
what is his doughy hand, kneading, needing
what is a fiery oven, the hateful dark
what is a little girl sent to the store
what is a heel of loaf left from the feast
what is a sack of crumbs for lovers' park
what is an old man at swan lake at dawn
what is my selfish want of you again
what is a cherry blackbird in the sky

Necropsy of Al Purdy

i bought Sex and Death from Al Purdy
after his last reading in Winnipeg.
he seemed twelve feet tall
as he stumbled onto stage
but his voice rang as solid
as the rock of ages:
the final democracy of dying
or the demo-sale of romantic love
his proud heresy against the old world orders
or the cheap price of poetry and draft beer.
he made me laugh,
but most of all he was that rarest thing, a reasonably honest man,
with a voice as clear as arctic water
in a wilderness of Canadian quiet desperation.
he paid a price for his big mouth, sentenced
to decades of wage-slaving in a factory for soft beds.
now the lumbering young nation's busy writing *spin*
to slake its thirst for another institution.

look, just listen to his words,
and enjoy the sound of one man.

transcona
(trainsong)

transcona's where the trains go
to settle and clean in the middle of our country
transcona's where i went that day we yelled and cried
i sat by a ditch in a field of chalk yellow
black birds left a tree
and i calmed slowly and remembered
how much i love you—
a red-engined freight train split
the horizon from the sky—
so i pointed my car home again, west
towards our house in the giant reaching trees
of winnipeg, but first i drove and drove
the dirt roads cut in squares
in the one space
all 'round transcona

transcona's where the trains go
to settle and clean in the middle of our country
transcona's thousands of rail cars
in the continent's biggest yard
with space for hard-working people
in the west, where the sky
makes your heart better
there's room for your elbows
and your dreams, a sun-baked trail
beside the most beautiful field you've
seen, and metal tracks that shine
in long lines
into the dry and distant afternoon

transcona's where the trains go
to settle and clean in the middle of our country
transcona's where i ran to
        that day we split open
thank you transcona,
for bringing me home.

3

burning down the suburbs

burning down the suburbs

the Earth Liberation Front's burning down
the suburbs where I played green and sleazy,
the marshaled lines of armoured s.u.v.'s,
the uber homes the middle gentry own
on the edge of dark's wilderness, the brown
grass, the apple boughs falling to their knees,
I ran, famous among our crab-like trees.

(democracy? please speak into the clown.)

I read on Sunday cows are still alive
when hanging upside-down, their limbs sawed off
eyes bellowing to the twenty-year man,
it didn't used to be like this, he cried,
I'm sorry, if I quit my pension's lost,
please chain my feet, cut off my broken hands.

Babette

(in the window of the Kensington Bakery)

I heard you leapt from the Bloor Street Viaduct, a year after that well-lit winter moment in the window of Kensington Bakery.

You were about to leave, your small hand on the door, but stopped when you saw me and your face lifted and smiled gently, and I saw you too, and I think I actually sneered. Anyway, your fallen face, you ran off and I will never see you again.

I was twenty six when I shot half a black & white film with you playing a tramp clown—alone on a leafy bench in Cabbagetown's graveyard, or the best was a long shot of you clowning with some real old barnacles of Parliament St., you trying to juggle light gray oranges and them clapping you on. It was in this reel that I noticed your limp, I thought you were acting until I saw later your special shoe, why hadn't I noticed?

But Michael, my old friend and your old lover, forty-one to your eighteen, became convinced I had designs on you, and he convinced your father too, who was a year younger than him and who designed custom children's playgrounds for an international clientele. Michael watched my technique and told me I'd never be a great filmmaker, and my little story of a home-less man freezing to death in the rich Toronto sunshine was never done. The last shot would have been your feet dragging in the snow.

I moved back to Montreal and Michael wanted to come too and be roommates because you were going to school there. You'd come by that cold apartment, convinced too then that I wanted you when I did not, I was worried because Michael was hinting at killing himself, as he was losing you and it was plain his huge adult grief was infecting you like a slow, yellow poison. The day I asked if you were all right, you doubted my motives, and look at me with his borrowed eyes. I gave up.

The spring came finally and you both moved away and there was a tidy white noose left behind on the floor of Michael's clothes closet. Too late to be a cry for help, just his way of spreading it around.

There was one colour reel too, a close-up of your face in makeup against the pale green lettering on a grocery sign, every expression we could think of: cartoon joy and grief, suspicion, fear, doubt and loneliness, your giant vermilion mouth and piercing black-rimmed eyes. I mailed that reel to your father. He has it now.

I'm sorry for that forever frozen moment in the window of Kensington Bakery. I can't know what kind of a seesaw you were on by then, but I placed my hand on one side of it that day.

F-movie

(cartoon+live action collages)

dancing F's
F's in signs, many
F's mounting each other like dogs in a dewy playground
huge F's in the sky
F's moving like stalking insects
zooming clumsily into & away from F's
F's everywhere, crowds of F's on sidewalks, F'cars @ rush hour
F's falling like snow.

oshawa

i went to oshawa but i'd already been there
it was the same as 900 other places

the same wall-eyed cats & round-eye politics
back street hawkers & main street hookers
buried burial grounds & poisoned fish streams,
& the same love dreams

the same flag colours and safe-as-houses
rush hour drones' bold-fingered instructions
convenience store kids & pancake diners,
walmarts, money marts, one big bank
middle managers openly weeping
the open sores of the worked-over classes,
my own fitful sleeping,
richness in churches & poverty of spirit
wonder-breaded mornings & milk dud minds,
& the same come-on lines

the same lonely bus drivers in a swoon
good mothers hanging on
& men fucking nowhere
children i'm-getting-out-of-here anyway i can
government confidence men & hypnotists for hire,
more private puppeteers pushing your buttons and pulling your string,
of course, the queen of all the empire,
always, the same exorbitant exit fee,
& the same tv

i went to oshawa but i'd already been there,
it was the same as 900 other places

Canada Day

(found poem — St. Laurent & St. Catherine, Montreal, July 1, 1995 —
to be sung & tapped to)

bonjour bon prix la biere froide et les femmes chaude
sexe non stop sexe plus sexotheque boutique videoX strip teaseuses—
cinema-eve palais d'amusement animatrice pour couple
peep show dans le cinema vrrrraiment le plus hot en ville
venez goutez-come and taste
bonne fete-happy Canada!

Your Brown Shirt

I pulled up your brown shirt
And down your blue pants
You were pink, like a pearl
And I was green as an Irish ass

You kissed me on my chest
And arms, and the inside of my legs
And you knelt and brushed yourself
Across me and hugged my little head

For hours that singlet night and blowzy morning
On my home-made bed
You opened up, your legs your arms
You spread yourself like bread

I tasted for the first time
Your butter and jam your salmon berry
Your currant drink, your black toast
Your single drop of honey

Yet each time I came to you
You stopped me at the gate
You finished yourself, and you finished me
And then it was late

peasant
(for john berger)

i am a peasant
in the way i look at you
in the way i grip my hammer
in the way i slaughter a love song

i am a peasant
in the way i eat my food
quickly and for an hour and with appetite
for the satisfaction of easing my earthly need

i am a peasant
because i feel awkward in a suit
and proud and strangely elegant in a suit
and i point to others as *suits*

i am a peasant
because a tie is a noose around my stiff rough neck
a dog's collar and a convict's chain
yet a red tie at a wedding is an open display of my life's blood

i am a peasant
and i work with my hands,
or a computer, or a steering wheel,
or a machine the size of a building

i am a peasant
and my hands are scarred, my back is bent
and this is normal
and i'm proud of this

i'm a peasant
because the look in my eye
instructs you not to trust
me if you require me to become you

Tell me the Truth
(for W.H.)

some say it's just a little boy
slinging rocks at a bird
some say it makes the world go round
and some say that's absurd
but when i asked the girl next door
where her long legs led
her boyfriend knocked me to the ground
and kicked me in the head

does it look like a pair of blackshirts
or a posh restaurant seen from outside
does it smell like a hospital
or can it be a comfort when it's on your side
does it sting just to think of it
or would you rather watch tv
but the news is always full of it
o tell me the truth for free

our history books show little else
that is, the war against the poor,
there's too many! they're bursting at the gates!
we'll send ours and you send yours
i've found the subject's rarely mentioned in
academic halls
but i've seen it scribbled on
their walls in bathroom stalls

does it howl like a giant collie
or boom-boom like a military band
it's the choice harpoon of the holy
it's the master's hand
is it a homeless riot
or is it watching, warm, from the pub
is it hitting your child till it's quiet
or is false-scarcity your club

i looked inside the summer house too
and it was waiting there
the borders that day were open to few
and only with the right eyes and hair
hate is fear, so look at that:
what are you afraid of?
yourself in the mirror with a baseball bat
now tell me the truth about love

genoa
(for carlo)

it's important to understand
when we make bargains with *polizia*
to protect us at night
in return for a blind eye,

when we ask the *governo*
to cleave off our hands
and sell them to mexico,

when we let leaders *d'affari*
lure us to their lonely chasms
in search of a ladder,

that when carlo died, he wasn't *da solo*
and neither are we, ever
as we shout our banner songs,

that we breathe the same *aria*
we are the same water,
teeth, bone—and shorn hair.

the day after st. patrick's day

. . . even though you don't drink 'cause you've poisoned your liver
and you won't tell jokes about how dumb you are
for the returning yank tourist while you dig a ditch and pray for rain
or maybe they'll buy you a pint—
it's the irish roaring in your ear,

they say there's more insanity (it's running in your family)
it's the magic, the black river just under the dayglo green surface
the power of five hundred fucking armies (europe's true religion)—
it's the irish roaring in your ear,

no more green beer or TV leprechauns magical lucky charms bullshit,
kiss me i'm irish, he says to my girl, *fuck off, so am I*—
it's the irish roaring in your ear,

let's all get shit pissed rat faced fucked up throw up
you're stupid and you know it you sing and dance
and finger your neighbour over the fence and over the water
the sugary taste of a good hate—
it's the irish roaring in your ear . . .

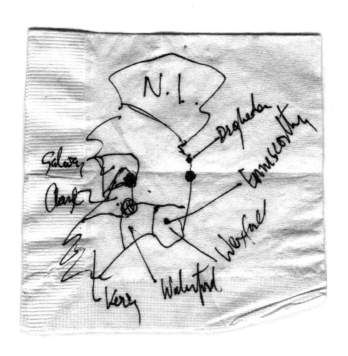

mad cows of england

feed yourselves, he said, pointing to the plain
the people ran and ate and coughed up bile
you see the red grass was modified
for only those with registered genes,

the owners laughed at their success
and forced the farmers to plunge their seed,
37%, the projected need of persons
to be culled to straighten the stock,

their bodies stacked and burned
in vales of orange pyres,
and then they smelled the new disease,
blowing across the fields of england

crow
(animation)

man

(animation)

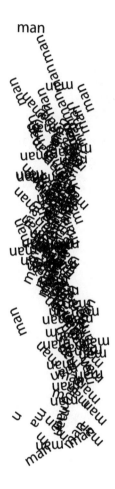

dogs
(animation)

tying their hair

tying their hair and singing loudly

tying their laces and laughing bravely

tying their bows and speaking rapidly

tying their knots and hiding quickly

tying their belts and kneeling gravely

tying their scarves and glancing secretly

tying their parcels and running terribly

tying their tops and lying lazily

tying their pants and kicking skillfully

tying their sandals and walking languidly

tying their skirts and twirling openly

tying their dresses and covering lightly

tying their feet and weeping quietly

tying their suits and swimming swiftly

tying their boots and working honourably

tying their breasts and breathing shallowly

tying their hands and praying nightly

about clive holden

Clive Holden is a poet and media artist living in Winnipeg, Canada. His publications include: *Fury - Fictions & Films,* (book, Arbeiter Ring Publishing, 1998) and *Trains of Winnipeg* (audio CD, Cyclops Press/Endearing Records, 2001). His film poems have been screened at the London International Film Festival, the Poetry Film & Video Festival in San Francisco, Vancouver's Video Poem Festival, Le Festival du nouveau Cinéma et des nouveaux Médias de Montréal, and the ZEBRA Poetry Film Awards in Berlin. This book is part of an on-going project, including a feature length experimental film (mid-2003), that is being collected at: www.trainsofwinnipeg.com.